The Secret Thoughts of Trees

Drawing & Poems
by
Storm

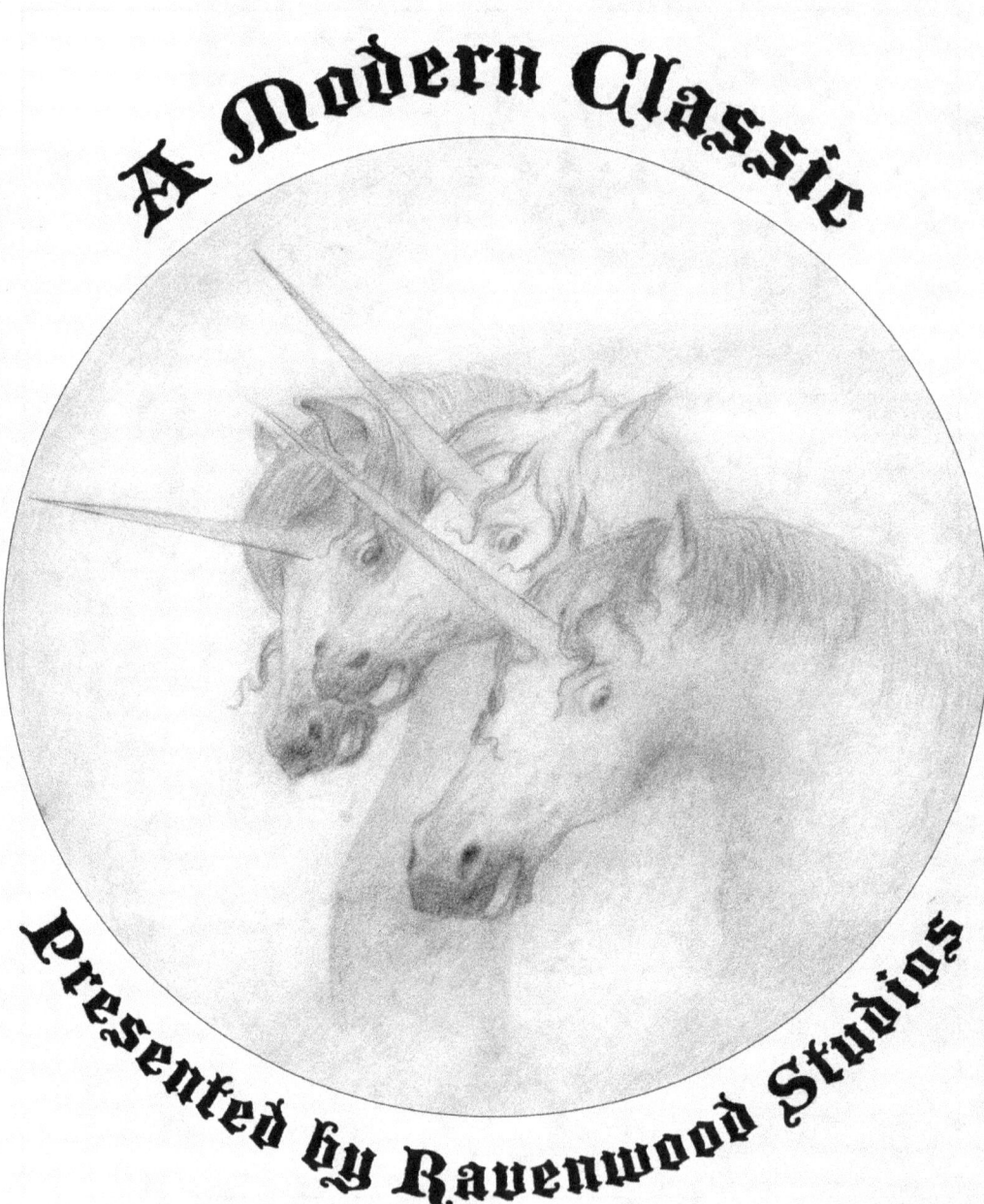

A Modern Classic

Presented by Ravenwood Studios

The Secret Thoughts of Trees

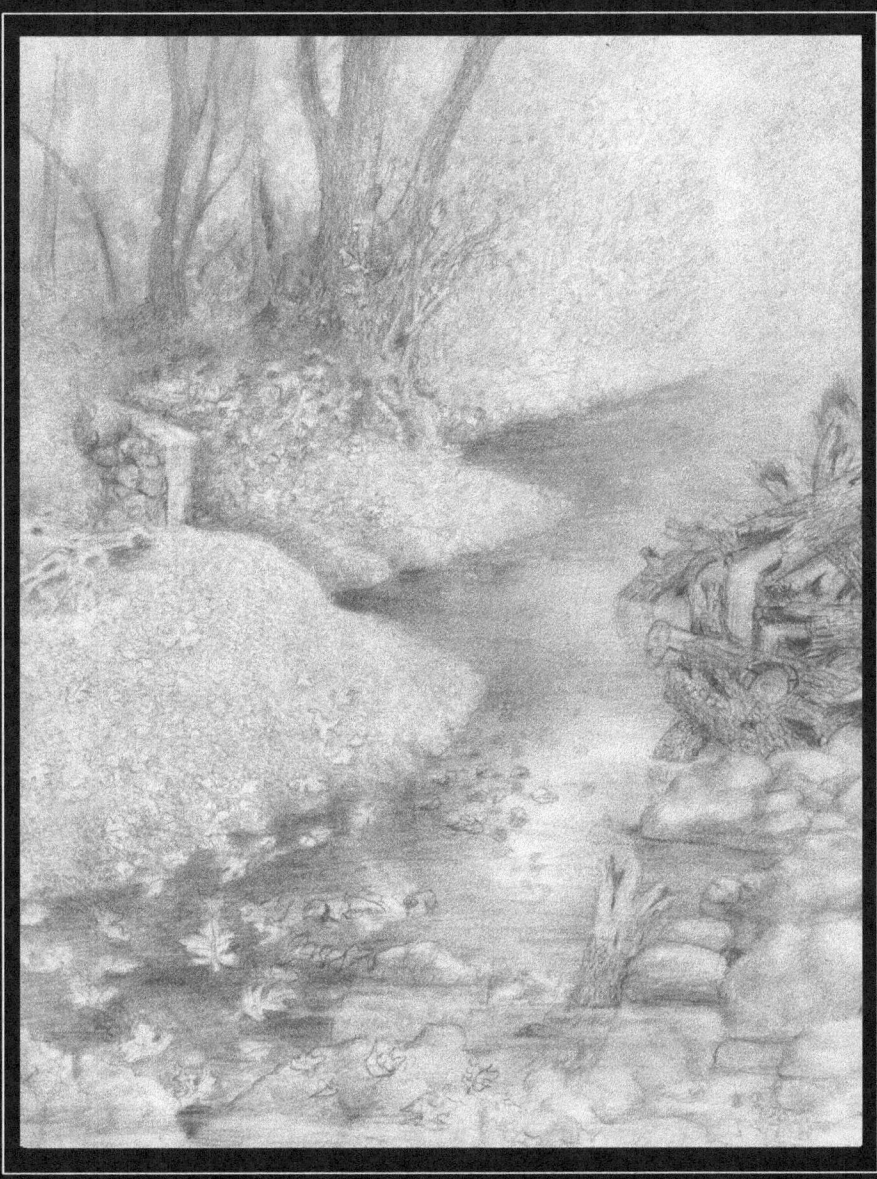

www.ArtWorkByStorm.com

ONCE A TREE SAW A HAWK FLY BY
HE WAS SO FILLED WITH ENVY THAT HE STARTED TO CRY
BUT WHEN HE TRIED TO FOLLOW ON THE WIND
THAT WAS THE LAST HIS FRIENDS SAW OF HIM

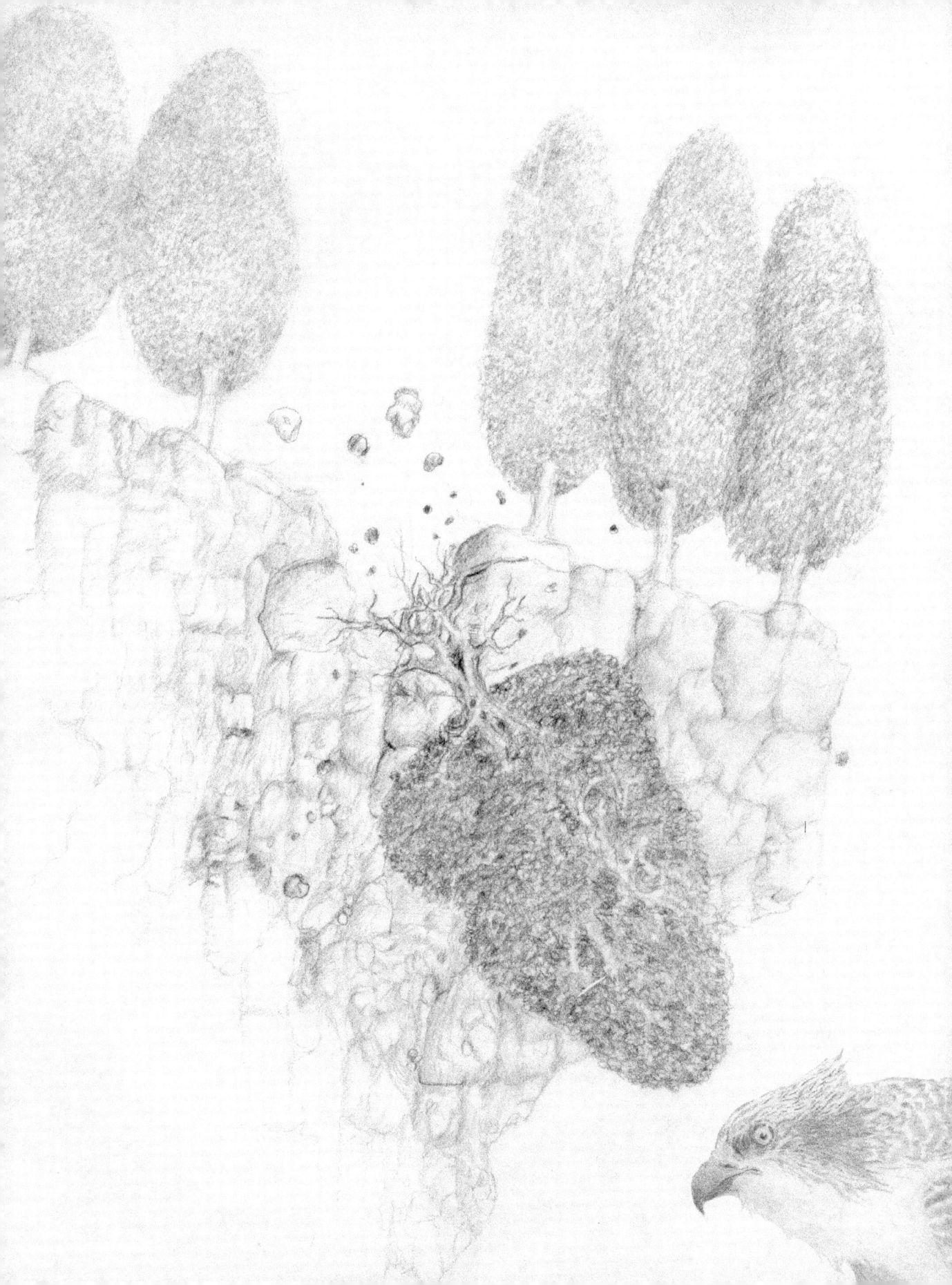

IF YOU WALK THROUGH THE FOREST YOU ARE NEVER ALONE

FOR MANY THINGS YOU CAN'T SEE STILL CALL IT THEIR HOME

SOME WALK, SOME CRAWL, SOME TRAVEL ON WINGS

YES THE FOREST IS HOME TO MANY THINGS

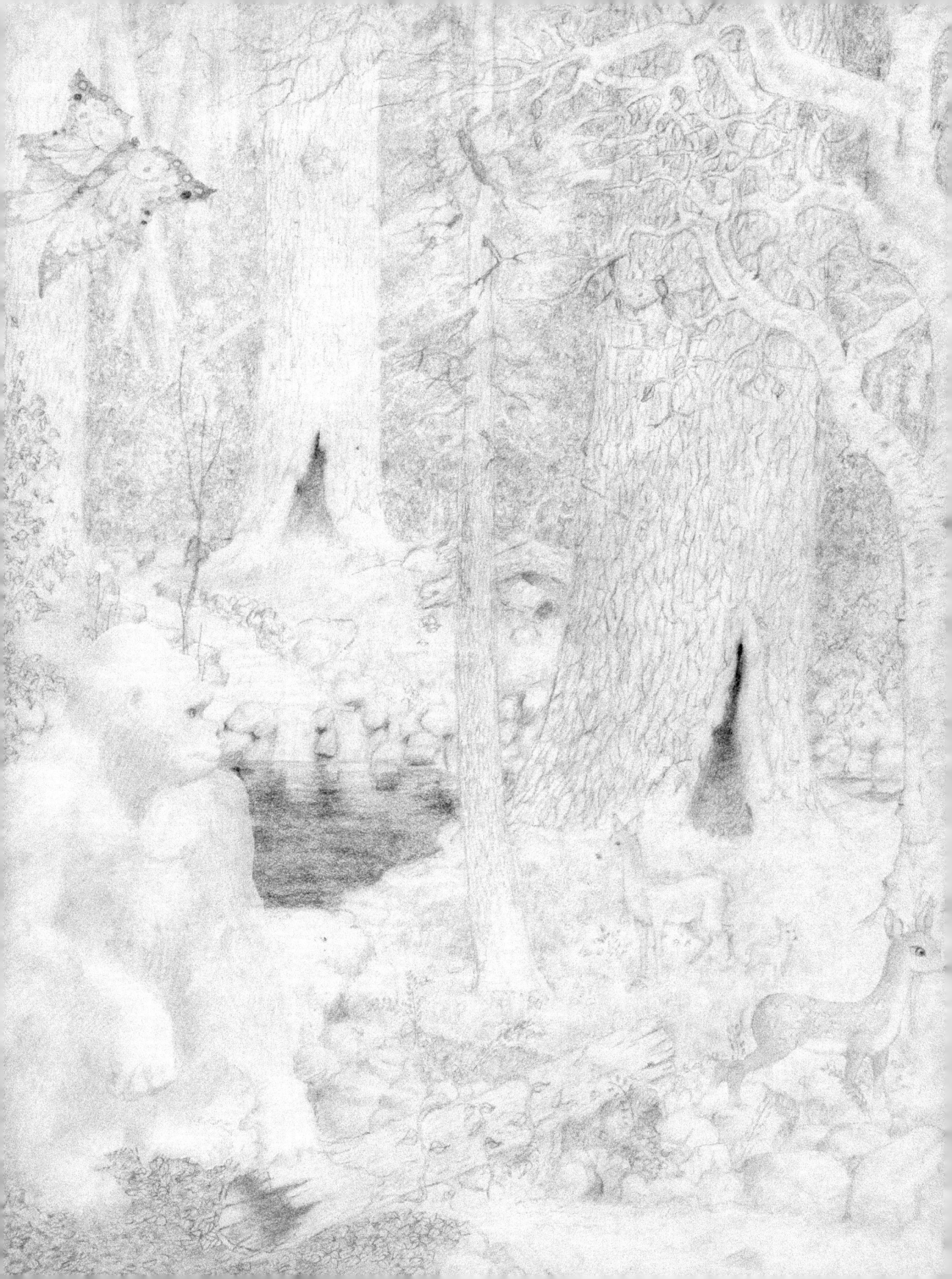

I STAND ALONE BESIDE TWO STREAMS
AND THOUGH I CAN'T TALK I STILL HAVE DREAMS
OF THINGS THAT YOU WILL NEVER SEE
EVEN THOUGH I'M JUST A LONELY TREE

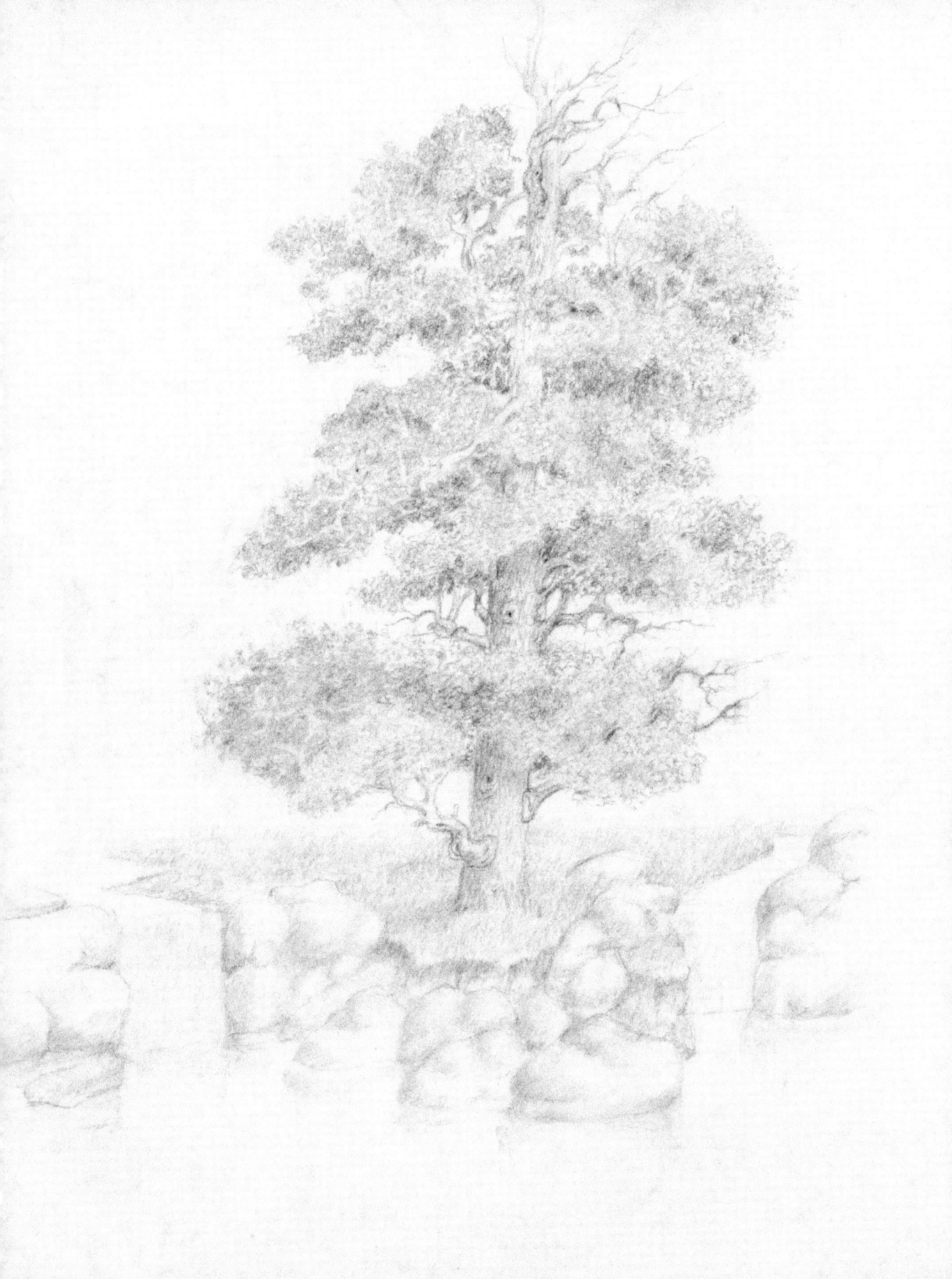

IF YOU SAID I CAN'T WALK THAT WOULD BE TRUE
BUT WHAT DOES THAT MATTER, I STILL HAVE A GREAT VIEW
OF ALL THE WORLD BOTH FAR AND WIDE
FOR HERE ON THE EDGE I DO RESIDE

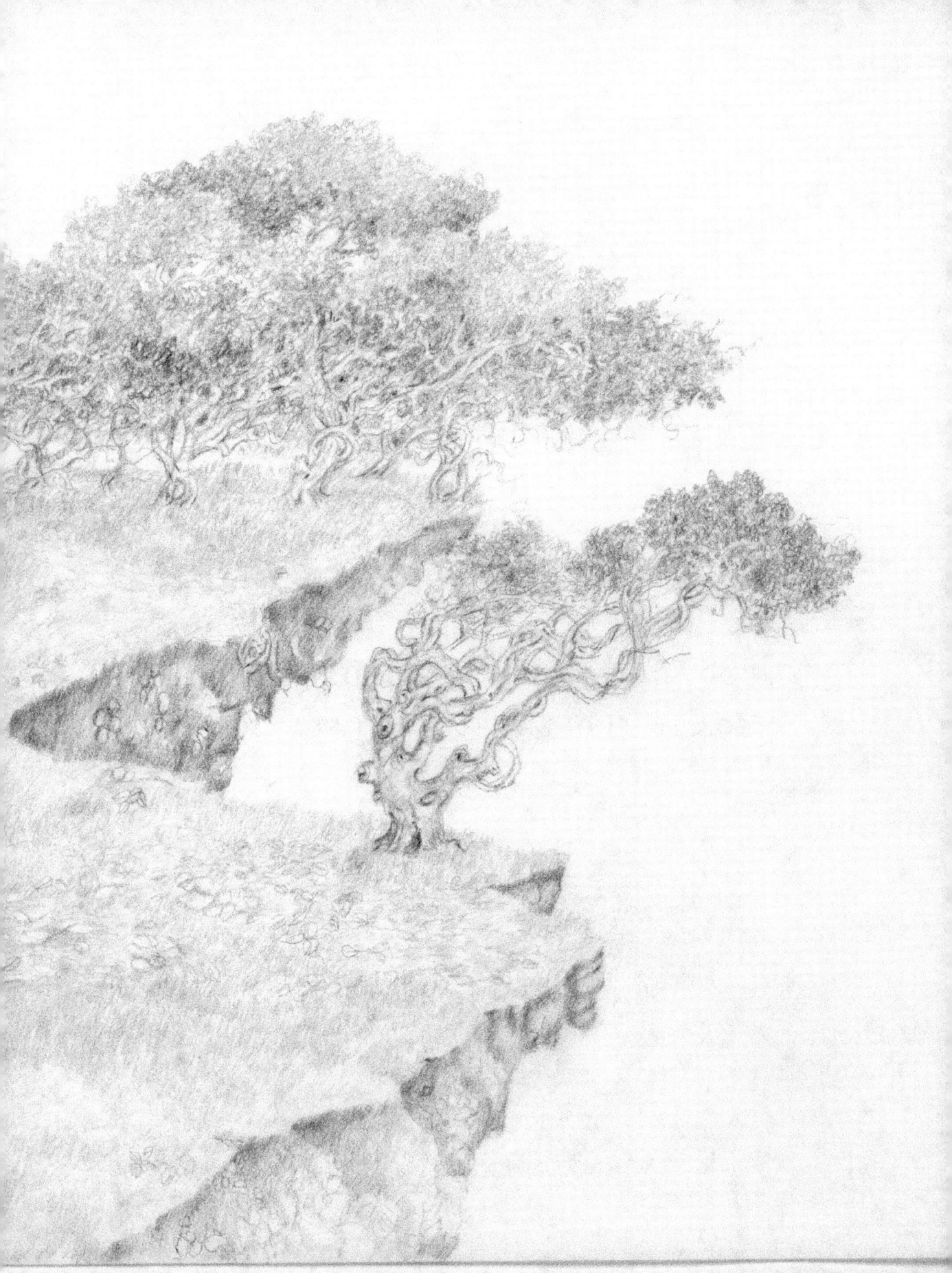

NOW HERE IS A SIGHT YOU WILL NEVER SEE
A TREE ON A ROCK FLOATING ABOVE THE SEA
IT DOES NOT MATTER IF THIS IS NOT TRUE
FOR TREES CAN ALSO DAYDREAM TOO

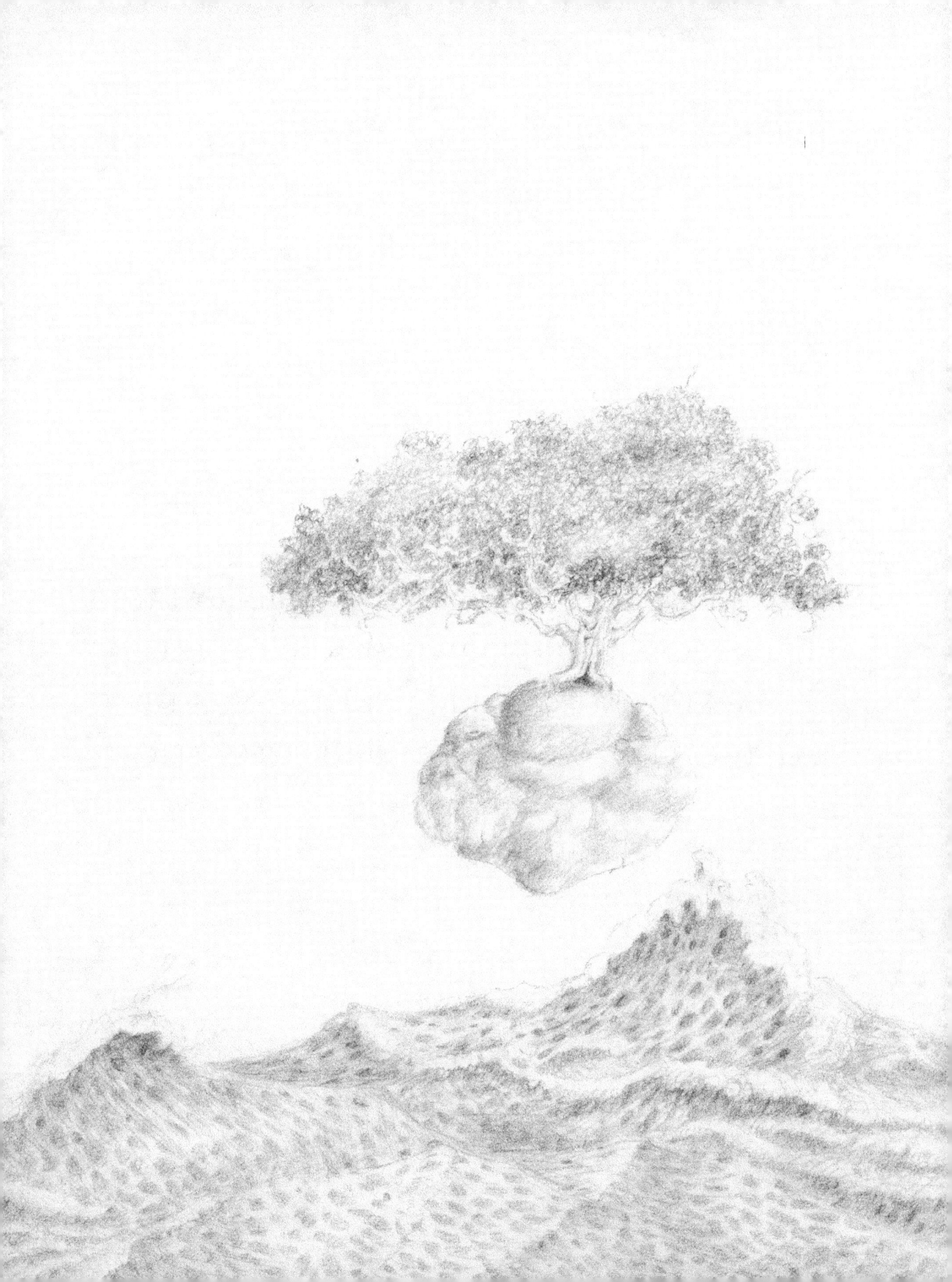

ON A SURF TORMENTED ROCK IN THE MIDDLE OF THE SEA
GREW A GNARLED AND TWISTED ANCIENT TREE
HE WAS THERE FOR BIRDS TO REST AT NIGHT
WHEN THEY GREW WEARY OF THEIR RESTLESS FLIGHT

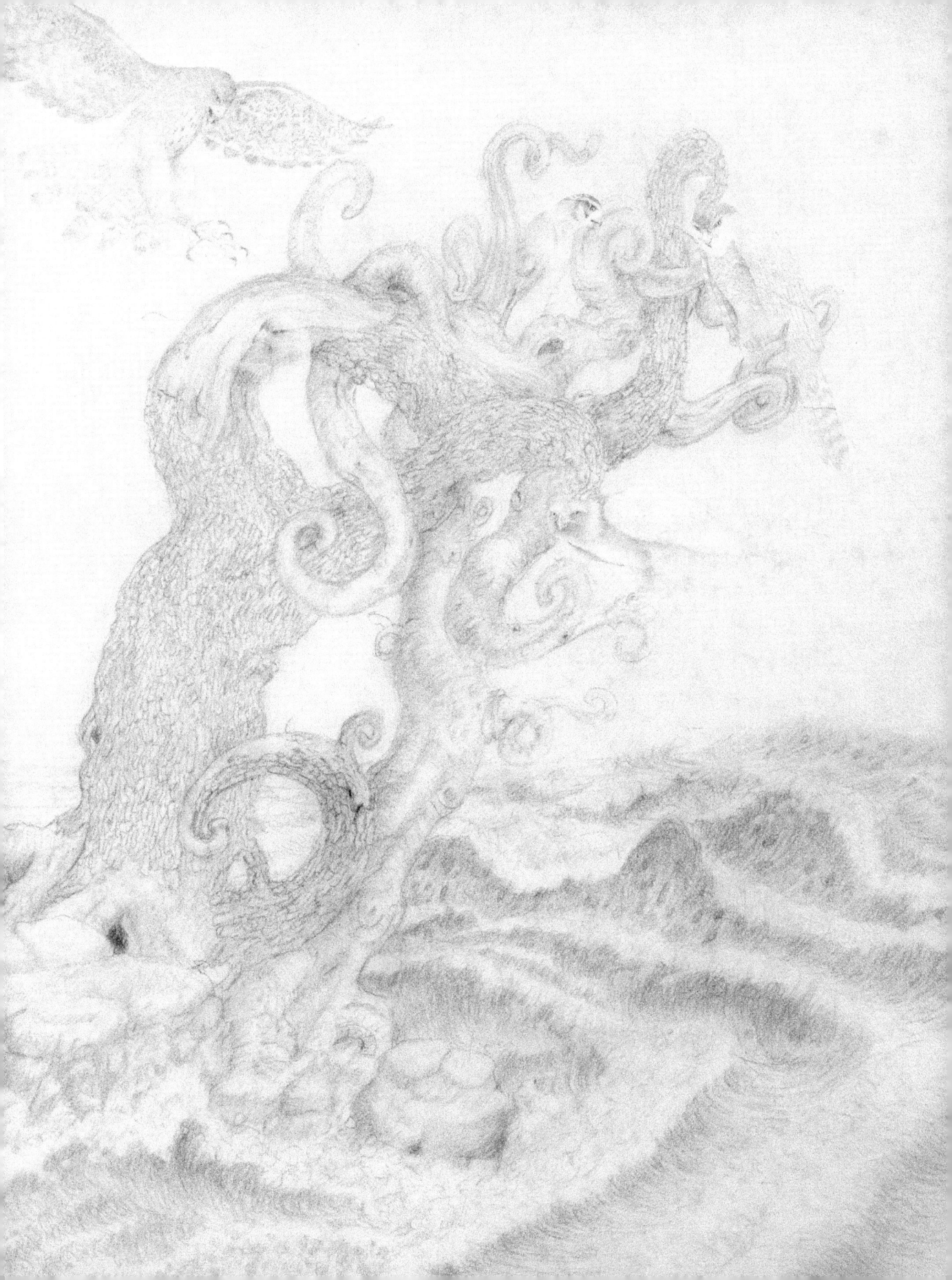

THESE TREES HAVE FALLEN WHERE THEY ONCE STOOD

AND NOW BECOME USEFUL FIREWOOD

WHERE ON A COLD AND DREARY DAY

THEY'LL HEAT A HOUSE WHERE CHILDREN PLAY

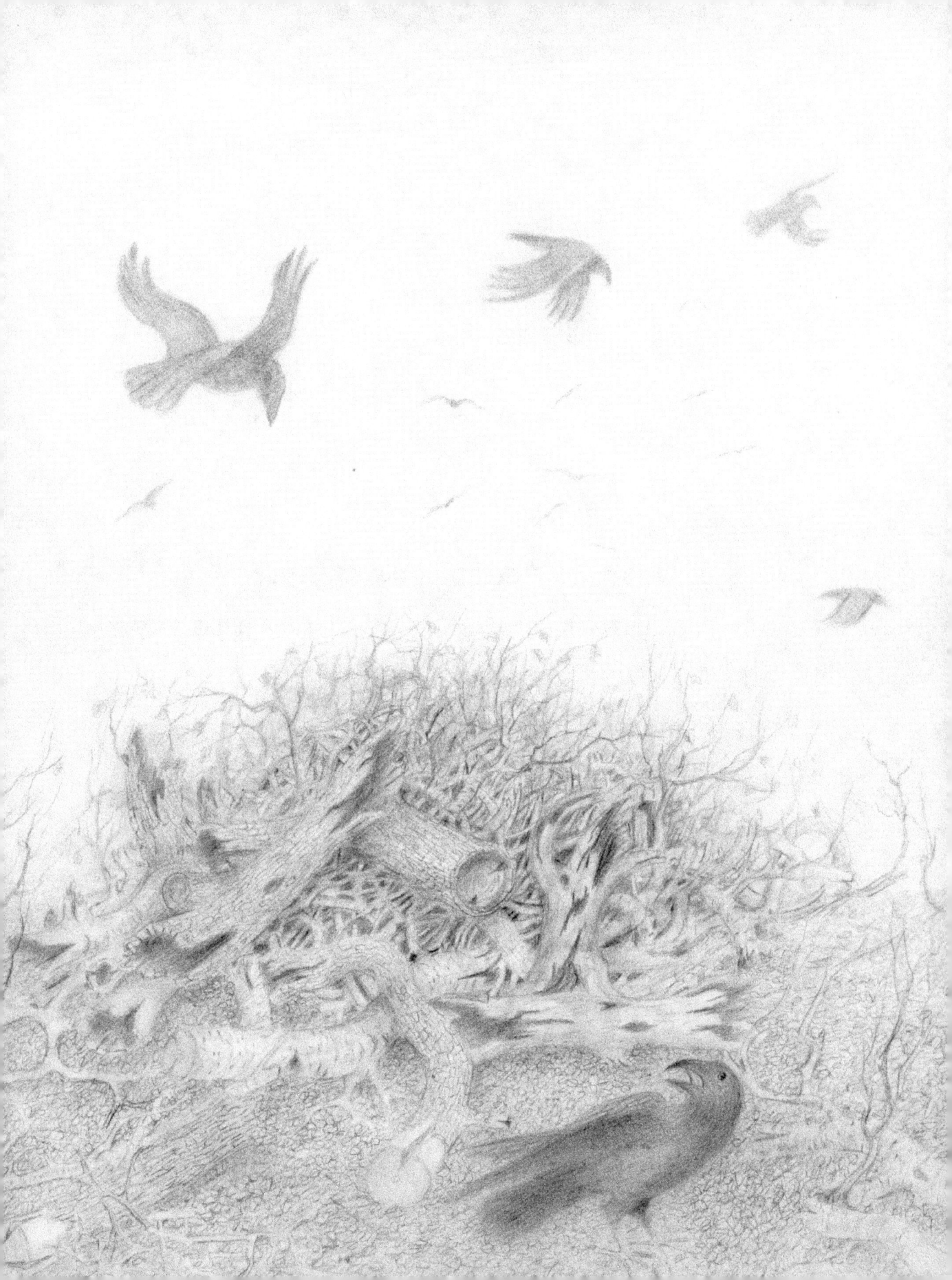

ON A BRIGHT COLD WINTER'S DAY
TWO SHIVERING TREES WERE OVERHEARD TO SAY
IF THERE IS SUCH A THING AS A REINCARNATOR
THEN LET ME BE REBORN ON THE EQUATOR

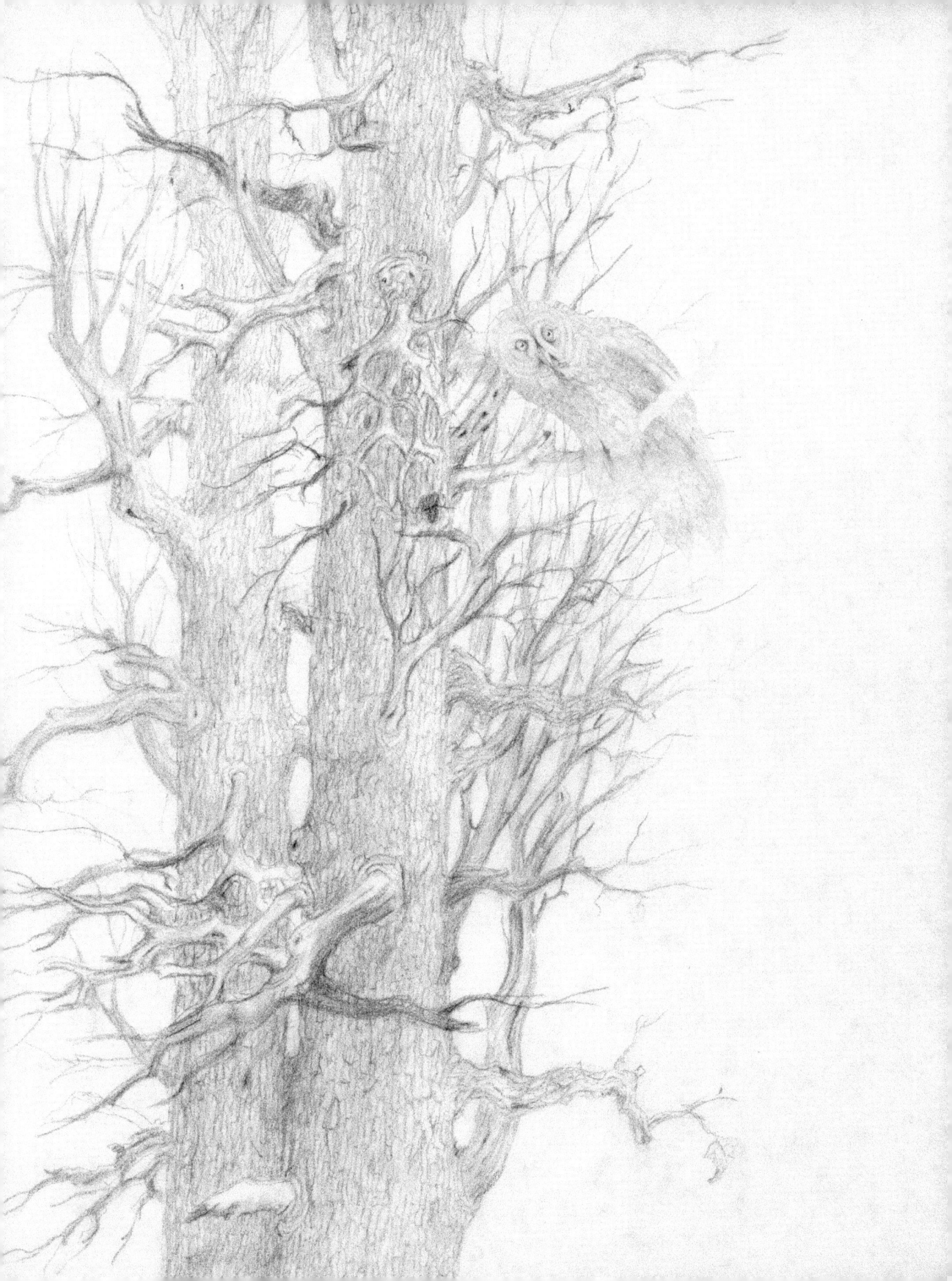

AMID THE HOWL OF A STORM AT NIGHT
THE ANCIENT OAK TREE HE HAD A GREAT FRIGHT
IT REALLY MADE HIM SHAKE WITH FEAR
THE SOUND OF THUNDER WITH LIGHTNING NEAR

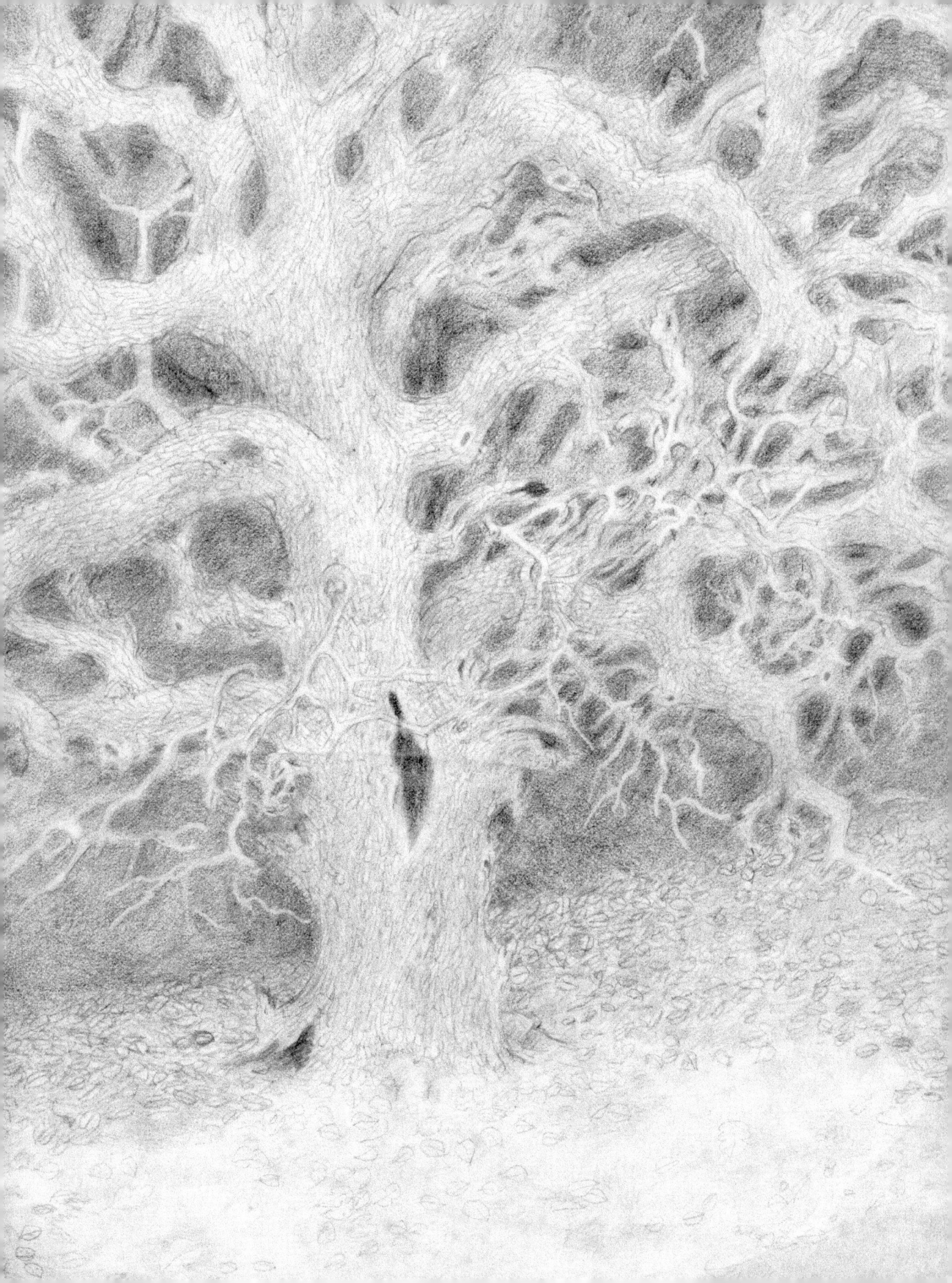

ON THREE HILLTOPS FAR AWAY
IF TREES COULD TALK WHAT WOULD THEY SAY
BENEATH THE SKIES WHERE BIRDS DO PLAY
"GEE, IT SURE IS WINDY OUT TODAY"

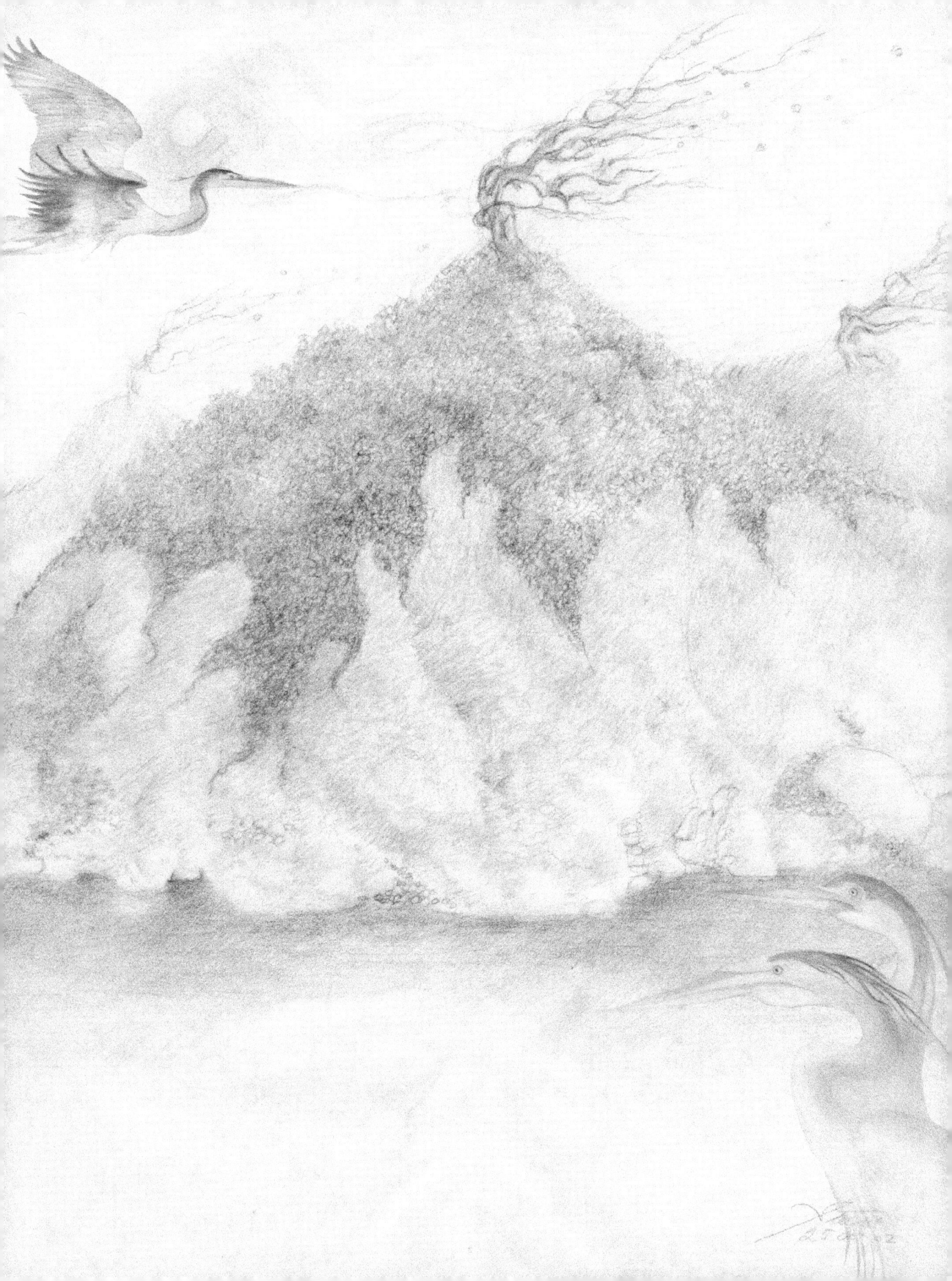

IF ALL YOU SEE

IS A PICTURE OF A TREE

THEN A CLOSER LOOK YOU MUST TAKE

FOR THIS IS REALLY A PICTURE OF A SNAKE

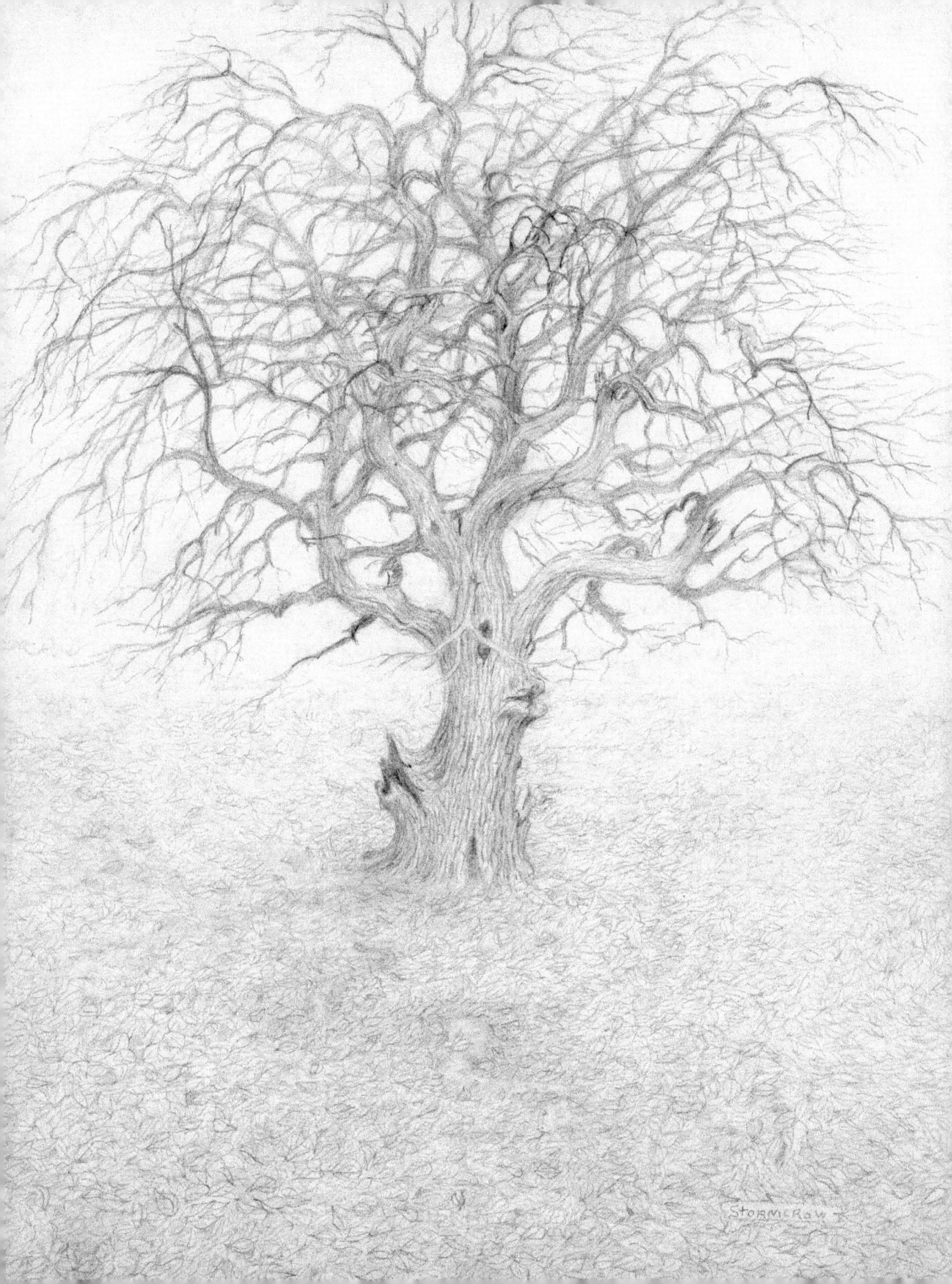

IF THIS TREE COULD TALK WHAT STORIES WOULD BE TOLD
OF ALL WHO HAVE JOURNEYED TO THE FORK IN THE ROAD
HOW DIFFERENT THE OUTCOME OF A LIFE
IF EITHER YOU TAKE THE LEFT OR THE RIGHT

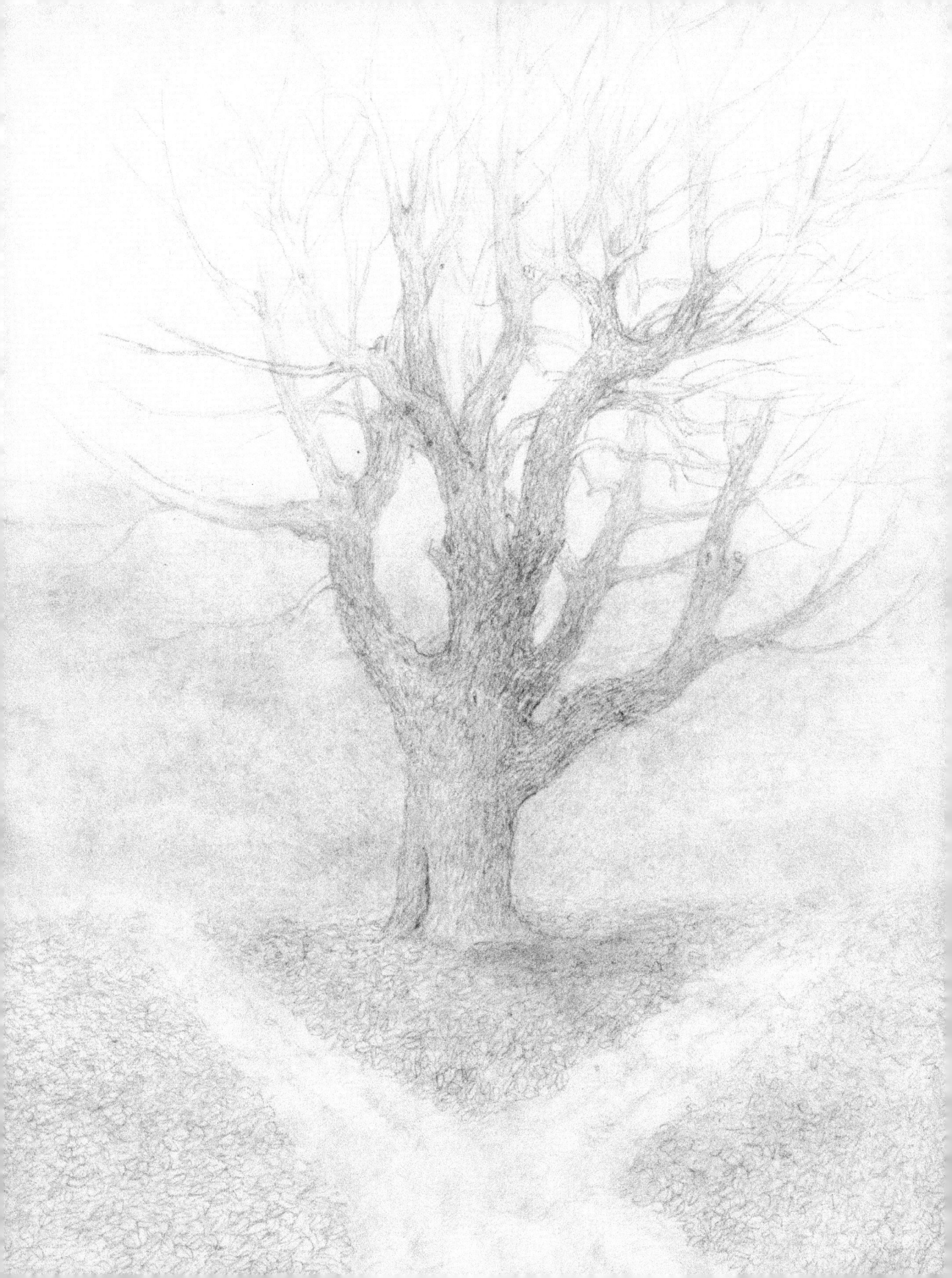

AND NOW THIS MIGHT BE A GREAT BIG "IF"
FOR WHO WOULD LIVE IN A HOURSE ON A CLIFF
EMBRACED BY THE BRANCHES OF A TREE
I THINK THAT THIS IS THE PERFECT HOUSE FOR ME

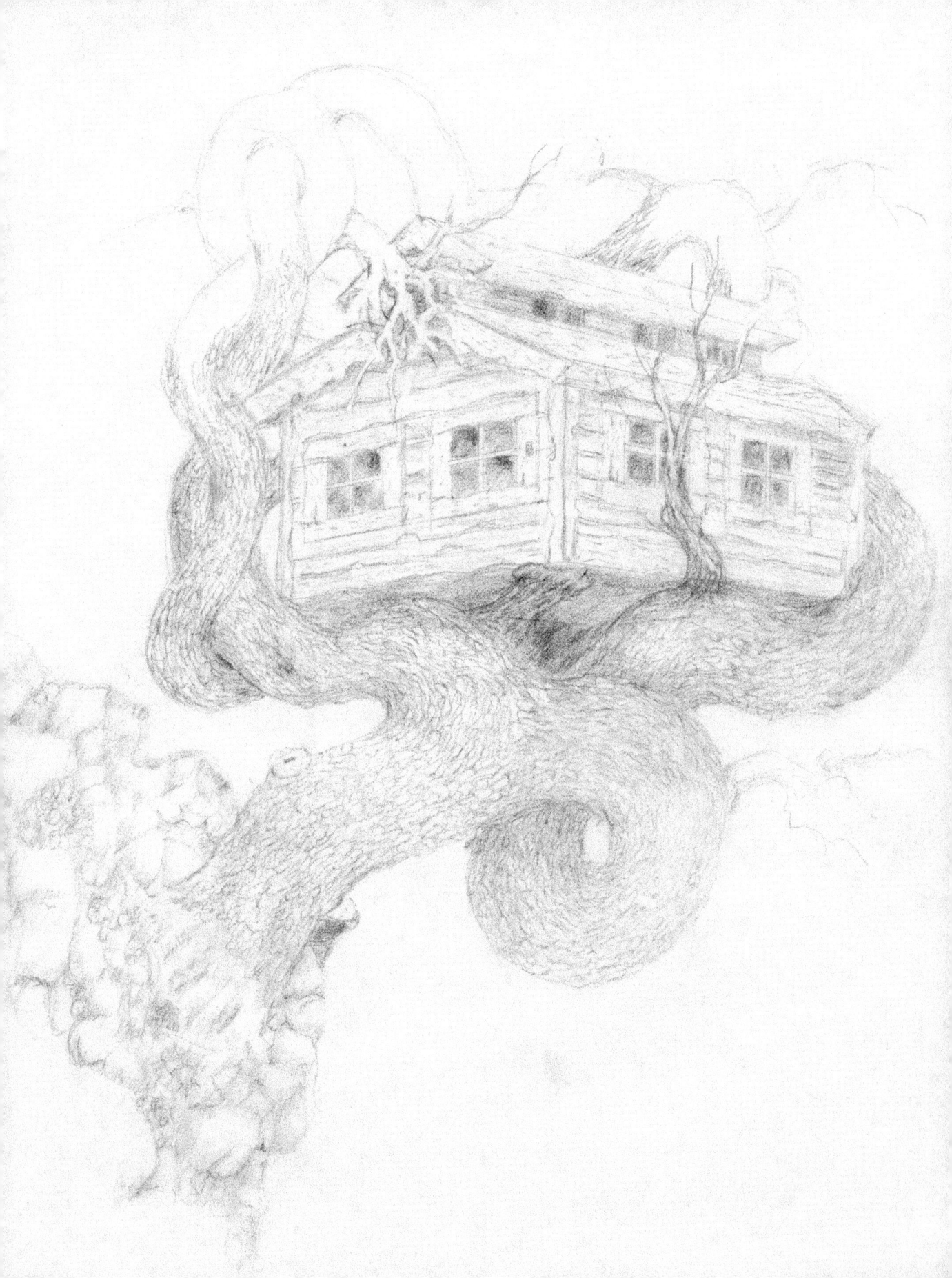

TWO TREES WHOSE BRANCHES SO ENTWINE
THAT THEY CAN STAND THE TEST OF TIME
THOUGH THEY HAVE NEITHER HANDS NOR FEET
STILL THEIR LOVE IS STRONG AND THEIR LIFE IS SWEET

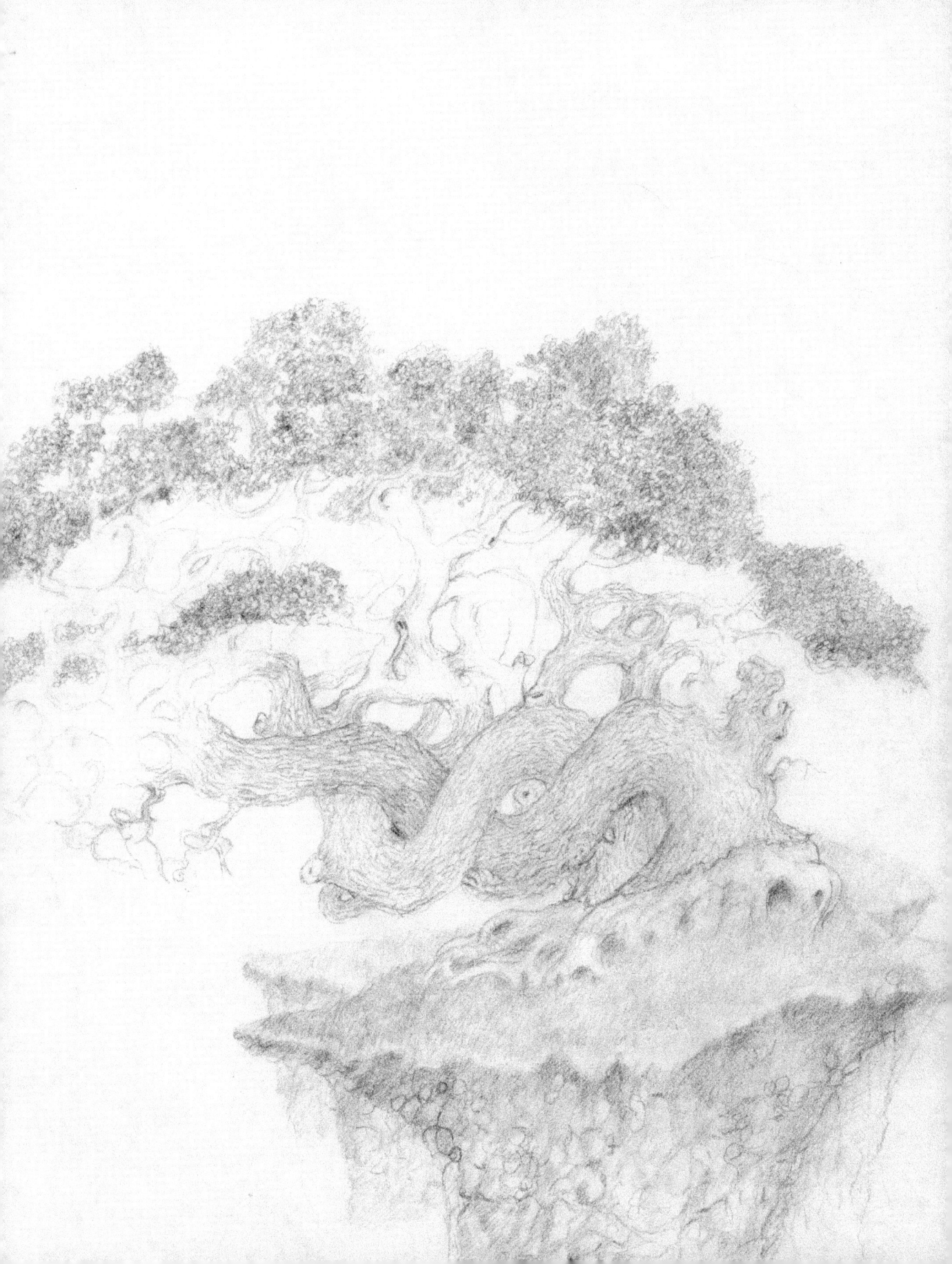

ONE BRIGHT MORNING IN THE MIDDLE OF THE NIGHT
THERE WAS AN AWFULLY STRANGE SIGHT
THAT IF YOU SAW IT WOULD GIVE YOU A FRIGHT
OF NEW TREES BEING BORN IN THE WEIRD MOONLIGHT

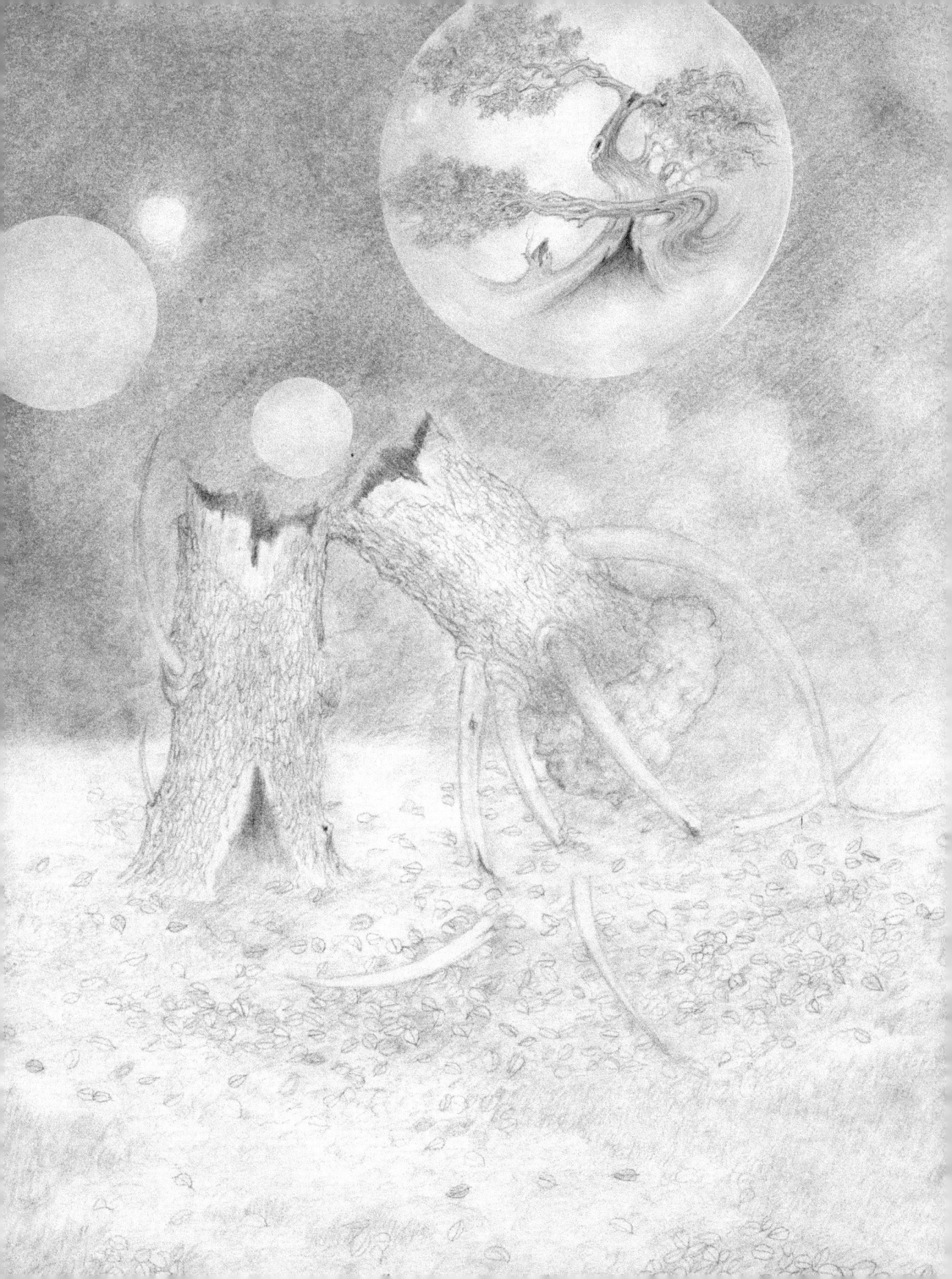

NOW YOU MAY NEVER SEE A TREE LIKE THIS

BUT THAT DOES NOT MEAN THEY DON'T EXIST

BUT IT IS NOT REALLY A CAUSE FOR SORROW

FOR IF YOU DON'T SEE IT TODAY, YOU MAY SEE IT TOMORROW

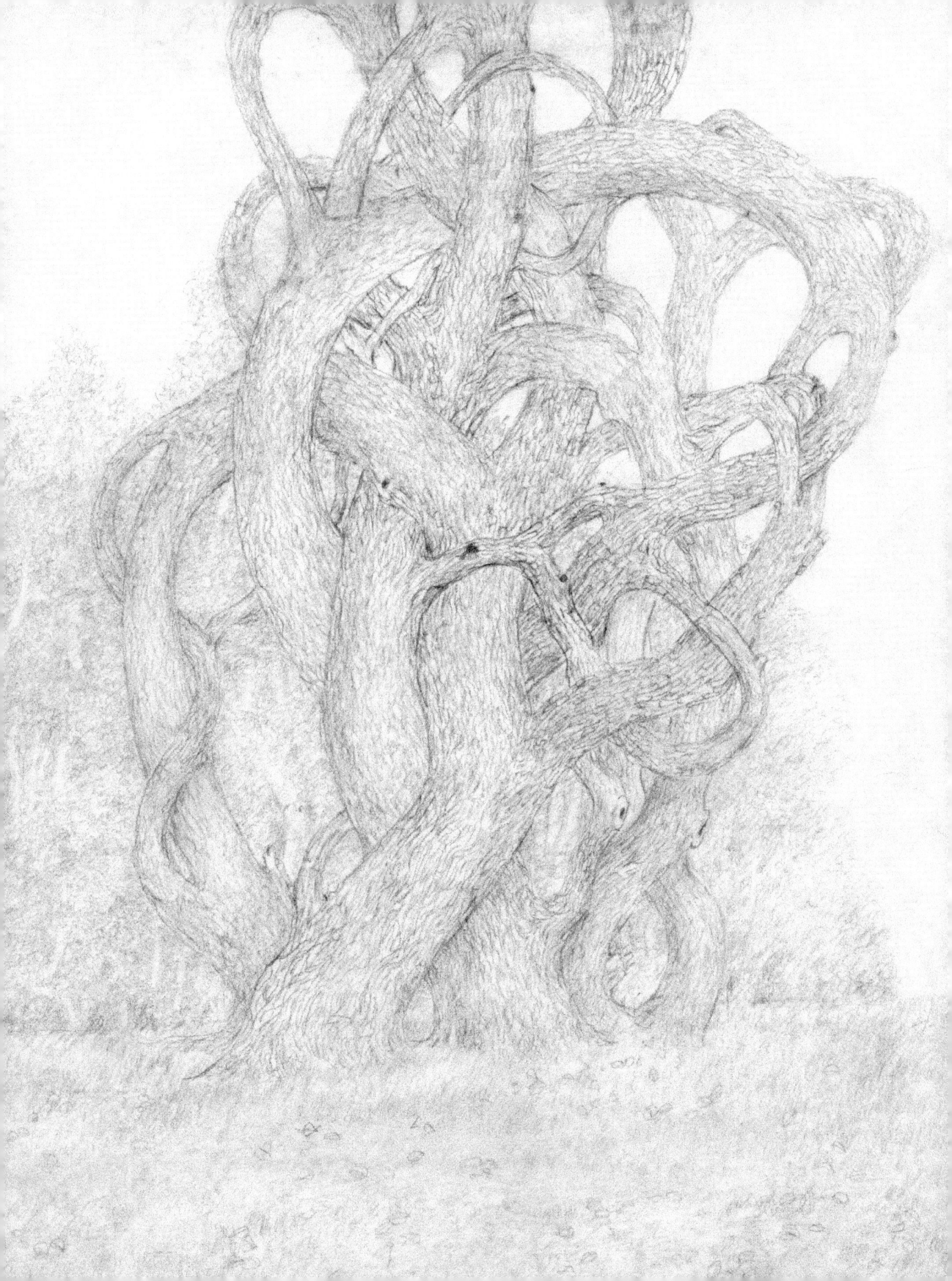

The End